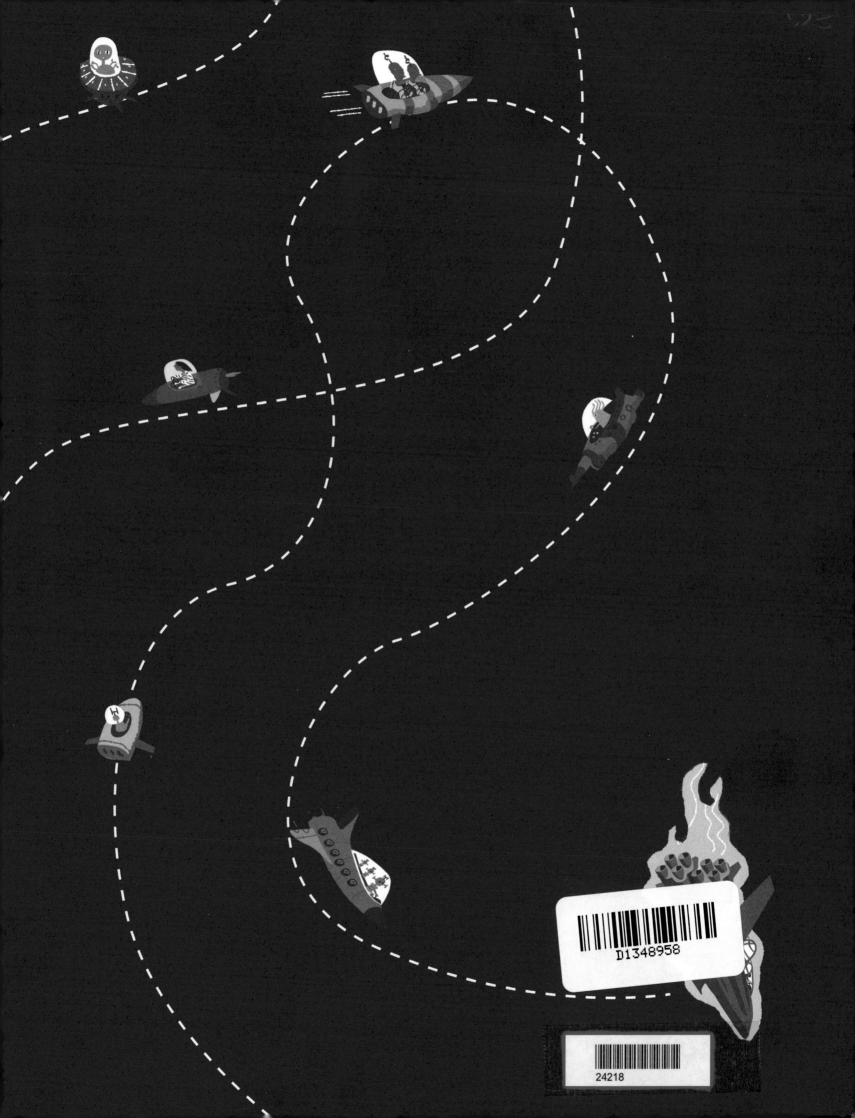

YOUR MISSION

The Zeebles need your help! Their rocket has crash-landed in Crater Canyon and they can't get home. Find your way to the crash site by choosing which exits or entrances to follow on each page.

1

Choose your transport

Jet Pack

UFO

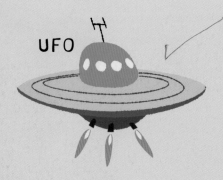

Space Camel

2

Trace a route

There are lots to choose from and you can go **BACKWARDS** and **FORWARDS** along the same tube.

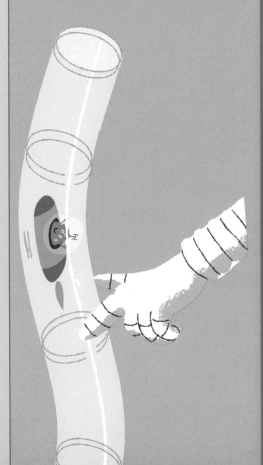

3

Collect on every page

Choose **ONE** of the missions below to help the Zeebles. You will find one of each object in every scene.

COLLECT 12 ZOBOGLOB BATTERIES to power up the engine.

COLLECT 12 CANS OF GLOOPY GLUE to mend the panels.

Collect 12 SPACE SPANNERS to fix the rocket's wings.

4

Use the book LIKE A REAL MAP

Turn the pages and use co-ordinates in this book just like you would with a real map. You can find out more about co-ordinates on pages 4 and 5.

5

SOLVE maths puzzles

Along the way you will come across Zeebles who are lost or need your help. You will have to use your super maths skills to continue. You might be asked to count up to ten or to find a shape.

Welcome to outer space

Look at the map of space. Can you see where the Zeeble's rocket has crashed? That's where you need to get to. Let's use co-ordinates to help us describe where the rocket is on the map.

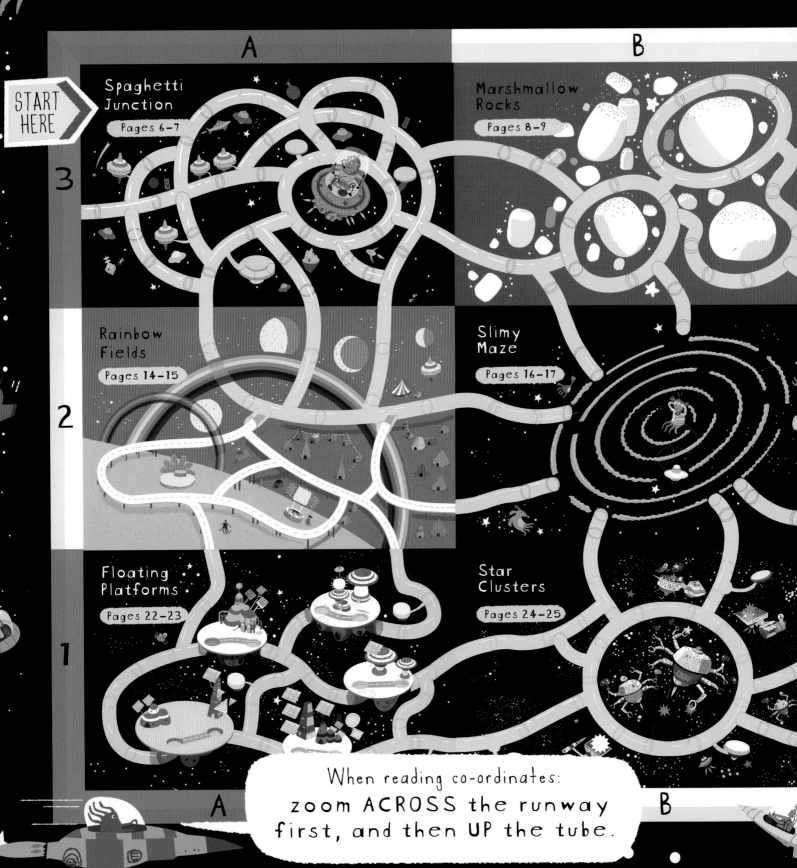

A B

START HERE

Spaghetti Junction
Pages 6-7

Marshmallow Rocks
Pages 8-9

3

Rainbow Fields
Pages 14-15

Slimy Maze
Pages 16-17

2

Floating Platforms
Pages 22-23

Star Clusters
Pages 24-25

1

A B

When reading co-ordinates:
zoom ACROSS the runway
first, and then UP the tube.

What are co-ordinates?

Co-ordinates are a set of letters and numbers that show where something is on a map. The letter comes first, followed by the number, so the rocket is in **(D,1)**. Look for the co-ordinate symbol throughout the book.

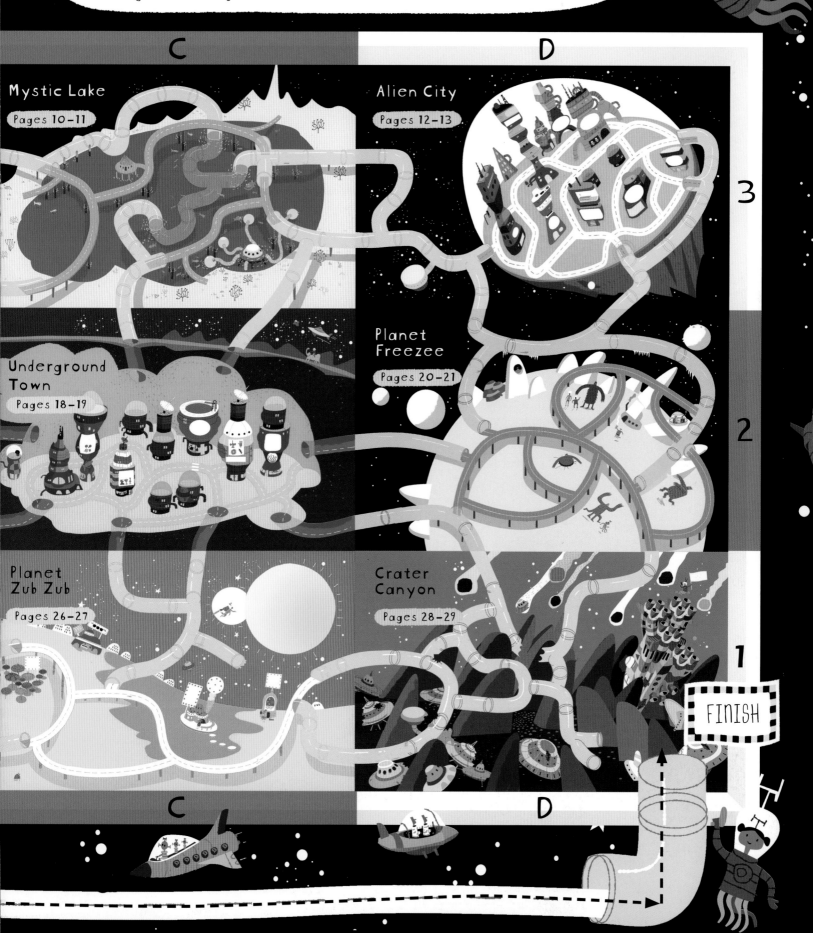

C

D

Mystic Lake
Pages 10–11

Alien City
Pages 12–13

3

Underground Town
Pages 18–19

Planet Freezee
Pages 20–21

2

Planet Zub Zub
Pages 26–27

Crater Canyon
Pages 28–29

1

FINISH

C

D

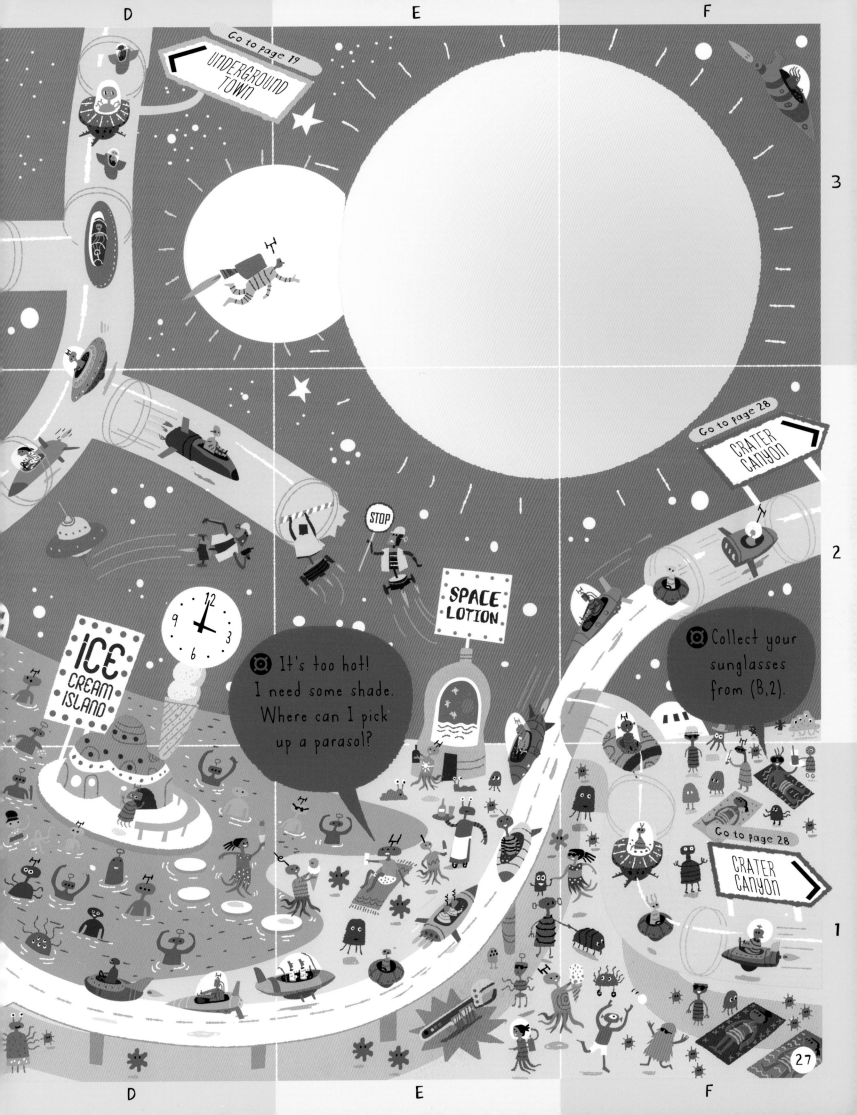

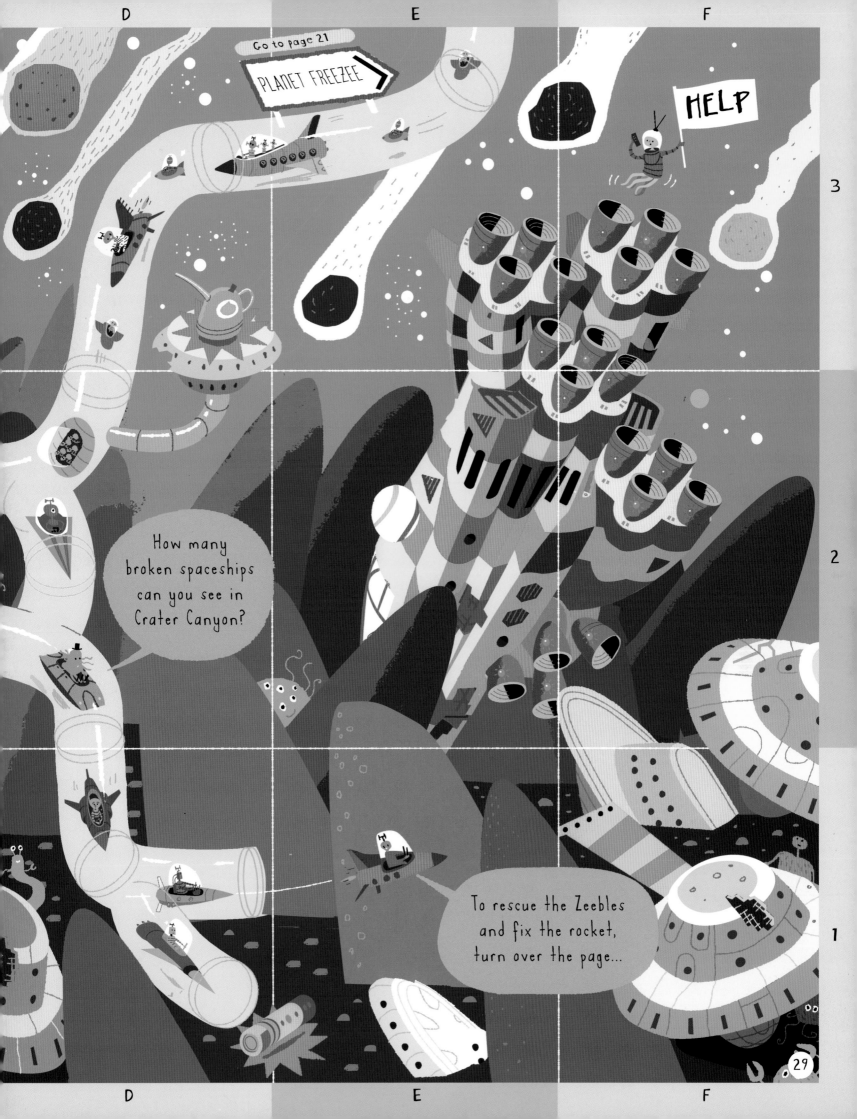

MORE FUN IN SPACE!

Understanding Co-ordinates

Encourage your child to look at other places where they might find co-ordinates, such as in an A-Z map book. Draw a map of space together and plot where you might put the stars and planets.

Counting

Go back through the book and look for more opportunities to encourage counting in space. For example, how many UFOs can you spot? How many asteroids can you see?

Telling the Time

Make a simple clock with your child to encourage them to look closely at telling the time. Use a paper plate, and attach arms using a split pin or pipe cleaners. Fill in the clock face using coloured pens. To go a step further, make paper 'flaps' which can be lifted up to reveal the minutes. Decorate to look like the Moon and stars, or the window of a spaceship.

Recognising Shapes

Make your own rocket! Cut out lots of different 2D shapes from coloured paper. You could use triangles for the nose and wings and a long rectangle for the body. You could even try using 3D shapes with cardboard boxes or plasticine.

Maths Problems and Vocabulary

Go back through the book and look for opportunities to build on mathematic vocabulary and problem solving skills. For example, if there are three Zeebles holding two ice creams each, how many ice creams are there altogether? Are there more pink stars than orange stars?

Length and Height

Using plasticine, make alien creatures with your child. How tall will they be? Perhaps they might have really long arms, and short legs. Line up your aliens in height order, with the shortest first.

Quarto Knows

Quarto is the authority on a wide range of topics.

Quarto educates, entertains and enriches the lives of our readers—enthusiasts and lovers of hands-on living.

www.quartoknows.com

Written and edited by: Joanna McInerney and the QED team
Consultant: Alistair Bryce-Clegg
Designer: Mike Henson

Copyright © QED Publishing 2017

First published in the UK in 2017 by QED Publishing
Part of The Quarto Group
The Old Brewery, 6 Blundell Street, London, N7 9BH

A catalogue record for this book is available from the British Library.

ISBN 978 1 78493 658 7

Printed in China

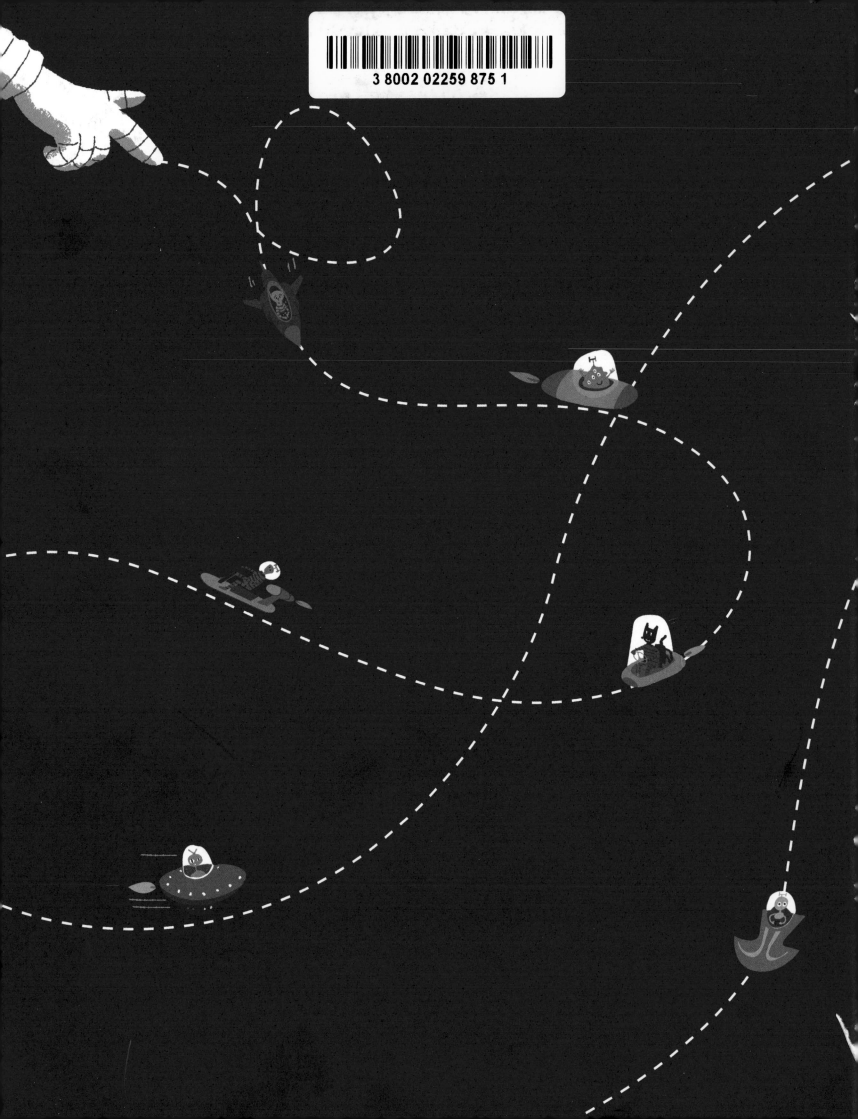